Rosa's Rescue

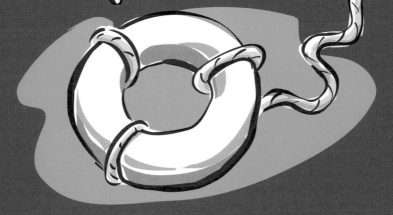

by Stacey Sparks
illustrated by Lisa Blackshear

Scott Foresman

Editorial Offices: Glenview, Illinois • New York, New York
Sales Offices: Reading, Massachusetts • Duluth, Georgia
Glenview, Illinois • Carrollton, Texas • Menlo Park, California

Rosa and her family sat in the car near the dock. They were waiting to ride the ferry. Rosa had not been on a ferry before. She had brought her camera with her. She planned to take a picture or two of her trip.

"How many cars fit on the ferry? Why do we have to pay so much money? How long does it take to cross the bay?" asked Rosa.

"You ask so many questions!" said Mama.

"How will we fit in that little space? What if we fall into the bay?" asked Rosa.

"Rosa!" said Papa. "Do not worry so much."

"What if the cars are too heavy for the deck?" asked Rosa.

"Do not worry," said the man. "The ferry is safe!"

"Are you the captain?" asked Rosa.

"I am the first mate," said the man. "I work with the captain. Sometimes I steer the boat."

"What is that noise? What was that funny feeling?" asked Rosa.

"We are starting to move!" said Mama. "The wind feels good!"

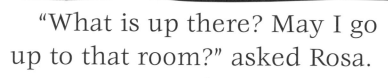

"What is up there? May I go up to that room?" asked Rosa.

"No. You need to stay here on deck," said the first mate. "The captain is up there. She steers the boat. She keeps the boat on course."

"You ask so many questions," said Papa.

"Look at the water," said the mate.

Rosa picked up her camera. She snapped a picture.

A boat came racing across the water. It was pulling a man on skis. The man waved at Rosa. Then, at that exact moment, he fell.

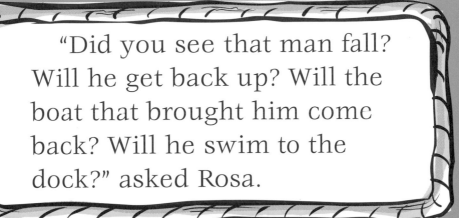

"Did you see that man fall? Will he get back up? Will the boat that brought him come back? Will he swim to the dock?" asked Rosa.

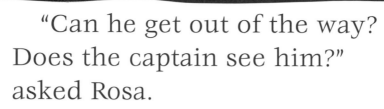

"Can he get out of the way? Does the captain see him?" asked Rosa.

"Run!" yelled the mate. "Tell the captain to stop. I will throw this to the man."

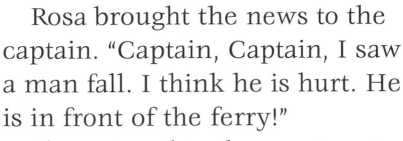

Rosa brought the news to the captain. "Captain, Captain, I saw a man fall. I think he is hurt. He is in front of the ferry!"

She pointed to the exact spot.

The captain turned the wheel hard. The engine roared. The ferry shook. Rosa held on tightly to her camera. Then the shaking stopped.

"Is the man okay?" asked Rosa.

Papa came into the room. "The man is safe," he said. "We pulled him out of the water exactly where you said. You have good eyes, Rosa."

"Good work," said the captain.

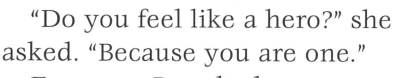

"Do you feel like a hero?" she asked. "Because you are one."

For once, Rosa had no more questions to ask.